T0132309

HOME
IS WHERE THE
HEART IS...

....

Lake of the Ozarks, MO

Written by Jamie Graham

© Copyright 2023 Jamie Graham.

All rights reserved. No part of this publication may be reproduced, stored in a retrieval system, or transmitted, in any form or by any means, electronic, mechanical, photocopying, recording, or otherwise, without the written prior permission of the author.

Order this book online at www.trafford.com
or email orders@trafford.com

Most Trafford titles are also available at major online book retailers.

 www.trafford.com

North America & international
toll-free: 844 688 6899 (USA & Canada)
fax: 812 355 4082

Our mission is to efficiently provide the world's finest, most comprehensive book publishing service, enabling every author to experience success. To find out how to publish your book, your way, and have it available worldwide, visit us online at www.trafford.com

Because of the dynamic nature of the Internet, any web addresses or links contained in this book may have changed since publication and may no longer be valid. The views expressed in this work are solely those of the author and do not necessarily reflect the views of the publisher, and the publisher hereby disclaims any responsibility for them.

Any people depicted in stock imagery provided by Getty Images are models, and such images are being used for illustrative purposes only.
Certain stock imagery © Getty Images.

ISBN: 978-1-6987-1562-9 (sc)
ISBN: 978-1-6987-1563-6 (e)

Library of Congress Control Number: 2023919672

Print information available on the last page.

Trafford rev. 10/17/2023

DEDICATION

I dedicate this book to my lovely sisters, The Lake of the Ozarks Developmental Center and Staff and to all of my Special Friends. Thank you for all the help and love you have always given me.

Special thanks to the Lake Ozark Daybreak Rotary who made this dream possible with their generous donation.

Foreword

Jamie Graham is a true inspiration to everyone he meets, including myself. His passion and love for life come alive through his art and writings and Jamie blesses those he cares about with the gift of his art.

Jamie is an advocate for those with developmental disabilities. He sees the ability... not the disability in others.

I love that Jamie chose to make this 4th book about the beautiful Lake of the Ozarks and Missouri and his life here through the years. His memories of the lake area are shared throughout this book and you can feel the love he has for his community.

Jennifer Campbell

One of my biggest accomplishments was
winning the Special Olympics
Hall of Fame Medal in 1997 for having

GOOD SPORTSMANSHIP
and for
BEING A GOOD HUMANITARIAN

MORNING
FISHING

Lake of the Ozarks is filled with so
many beautiful parks.

7

Ha Ha Tonka State Park was always a special family place that my mom held close to her heart.

I still love going there with all my special friends.

Ha Ha Tonka is filled with magnificent caves and many natural springs and walking trails.

11

One Of my favorite memories was the
TALL RED INDIAN
at Dogpatch near the Bagnhell Dam.
PROUD AND TALL
&

The Candy Shop next door was
YUMMY IN MY TUMMY
at Grandma's Candy Kitchen

As a teenager, I loved working

At FUN City USA. I was a groundskeeper and helped operate the train and sell balloons!

MERRY GO ROUND OOOOOOGOU

It was a BIG responsibility.

13

Riding on the bow of my grandpas boat on the Lake of the Ozarks was the

BEST.

Grandpa would pull me oh my surfboard..
FAST AND STEADY WE WOULD GO!

Bridal Cave draws people from near and far for the romantic atmosphere.

Many weddings have been performed there.

22

Printed in the United States
by Baker & Taylor Publisher Services